VISITOR GUIDES TO HAWAI'I

MAUI THIS & THAT

FACTS AND ANSWERS
TO THE MOST FREQUENTLY
ASKED QUESTIONS
ABOUT THE VALLEY ISLE

MUTUAL PUBLISHING

Library of Congress Control Number 2023940226

ISBN: 978-1-949307-53-5

Photos from Freepik.com: pg. 28 (humpback whale) © brgfx; pg. 39 (fruits) © pch.vector, (brewing equipment) © dgim-studio; pg. 40 © Freepik
Photos from Dreamstime.com: pg. 3 (background) © Wacomka, pg. 28 (taro) © Chuyu

Design by Courtney Tomasu

First Printing, September 2023

Mutual Publishing, LLC
1215 Center Street, Suite 210
Honolulu, Hawaii 96816
Ph: 808-732-1709
Fax: 808-734-4094
email: info@mutualpublishing.com
www.mutualpublishing.com

Printed in South Korea

Aloha!

ALOHA
is the spiritual key.

ALOHA is the familiar
Hawaiian greeting and farewell.

ALOHA signifies the sentiments of
affection, sympathy, kindness, and love.

ALOHA is the spirit of friendliness and
hospitality—the essence of the Hawaiian culture.

ALOHA represents the Hawaiians' love of life—
their art of living. For their wealth was not in
aggressive accumulation of things, but in their
joy in sharing and giving.

ALOHA to all of you who enjoy and appreciate
Hawai'i—its beauty, its people, and its spirit.

LaRue W. Piercy
Kailua-Kona, Hawai'i

Contents

Maui Nō Ka ʻOi

Maui nō ka ʻoi, translated as Maui is the best, is a well-known expression throughout the islands and although some may think it's just a marketing slogan to promote Maui tourism, the saying actually has its roots in ancient Hawaiʻi.

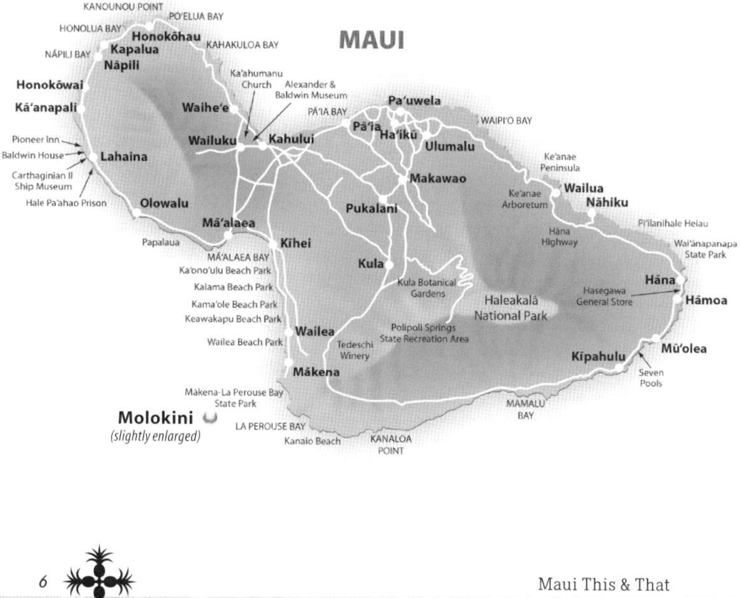

Maui

Name – 'Maui' is said to originate from the legend of Hawai'iola, who purportedly discovered the Hawaiian Islands several hundred years before their 18th century colonization. It is said that Hawai'iola named the island after his son, Maui, who was named after Māui the demigod.

Nickname – The Valley Isle. Most of the island's towns are nestled in the central valley between its two major mountain ranges: Haleakalā and the West Maui Mountains.

Flagvisioner, Wikimedia

Flag – Maui County adopted an official flag in 1990, which included a silversword plant symbolizing strength, spirit, and courage of the residents; ti leaves symbolizing the bestowal of blessings on the land; and wreath binding the four islands together. The four islands of the county appear in relative scale and were assigned different colors. The relevance of the colors is not known.

Color – Pink

Flower – Loke Lani (small rose)

FUN FACTS

- Maui is home to ten of the fourteen climates found on earth.
- Maui is the second largest of the Hawaiian Islands.
- Molokini Crater is one of just three volcanic atolls in the world.
- Maui is named after the demigod Māui.
- The Road to Hāna is the longest rainforest highway in the U.S. with 617 turns and 59 bridges.
- Maui is the best island for whale-watching with approximately 10,000 humpback whales migrating from Alaska to give birth in the warm waters of the South Pacific from December through April.
- Spinner Dolphins can be seen year-round in Maui!
- Maui is home to the world's largest dormant volcano, Haleakalā.
- ʻĪao Valley State Monument is a 4000-acre, ten-mile-long park surrounded by lush, tropical beauty.
- Maui has colorful sand beaches–black, red, white, and gold.

- Maui has the largest Banyan tree in the U.S. Imported from India, it was planted in Lahaina 150 years ago.
- Molokini Crater is home to over 250 marine species.
- Even though he didn't set foot on the island, Captain James Cook was the first European to see Maui.
- Lahaina was the Hawaiian Kingdom's first capital.
- The islands of Kaho'olawe, Moloka'i, and Lāna'i are all a part of Maui County, and once upon a time, they were all connected. This massive island was called Maui Nui.
- It snows on Maui sometimes! Usually at the upper regions of Haleakalā, but in 2019, Pōlipoli State Park saw snow during a strong winter storm.
- One of the tallest waterfalls on Maui, Waimoku Falls drops 400-feet down a sheer lava rock wall.
- Famous aviator, Charles Lindbergh, was buried on Maui in 1974.
- Founded in 1831, Maui's Lahainaluna High School is the oldest school west of the Rocky Mountains and was home to the first printing press in the western U.S.

PRECIOUS LAND

465,800 ACRES	
Farmland	242,688 acres
Rural	4,198 acres
Urban	24,078 acres
Conservation	194,836 acres

MAJOR LANDOWNERS (2017)	
State Government	122,208.7 acres
State Department of Hawaiian Home Lands	31,942.2 acres
Federal Government	33,660.3 acres
Kamehameha Schools	2,615.5 acres
Alexander & Baldwin	65,451.3 acres
Haleakalā Ranch	29,167.3 acres
Maui Land & Pine	22,354.9 acres
ʻUlupalakua Ranch	18,372.2 acres
The Nature Conservancy	7.9 acres

As of June 20, 2021, there are 67,761 acres of forest reserve land on Maui, 30,153 acres of private forest land, and five natural areas equaling 18,543 acres.

AGRICULTURE

Misc. fruits, tree nuts, berries–$16.1 million (2017).

Nursery, greenhouse, floriculture, sold, cultivated Christmas trees, woody crops–$13.1 million (2017).

Animals and animal products–$7.9 million (2017).

Maui's former sugar harvest

- One ton of water needed to make a pound of sugar–irrigation costs about $50 million for about half the crops–rest depends on rainfall.
- Crops average about 11 lbs. of raw sugar por acre.
- No insecticides used–biological control of 11 major insect enemies.
- Weed control by spray–hand, truck, airplane.
- Rats caused $2 to $4 million loss annually–diminished by trapping and poisoning.
- Production–over a million tons a year.
- Most of the raw sugar refined by California and Hawaii Sugar Co. (C and H), Crockett, California.

MAUI'S PEOPLE

Maui County Mayor: Richard Bissen

U.S. Representative: Jill Tokuda

Resident population of Maui was 164,303 in 2021 (including Kalawao County)

RESIDENT POPULATION BY CENSUS DESIGNATED PLACE 2016-2020	
Hāna	768
Makawao	7,989
Wailuku	17,523
Lahaina	13,216
Kahului	29,993
Kīhei	22,749
Pā'ia	2,285
Kula	6,687

85.4% of the population lives in urban areas

14.6 % of the population lives in rural areas

Aerial view of Kīhei. Forest and Kim Starr, Wikimedia

In 2022, the top three ethnic groups on Maui were Caucasians, Hawaiians/Part-Hawaiians, and Mixed (except Hawaiian).

Caucasians	34%
Hawaiian/part Hawaiian	23%
Mixed (except Hawaiian)	16%
Filipino	15%
Japanese	10%
Chinese/Korean/Tongan/other	1%

The median sales price of a single family home on Maui in from 2022 was $983,575. The median sales price of a condominium on Maui in 2022 was $820,000.

RELIGIONS

46.0% of the people in Maui County are religious:

Catholic	23.4%
Another Christian faith	4.8%
Church of Jesus Christ	4.8%
Pentecostal	4.8%
An Eastern faith	4.4%
Presbyterian	1.4%
Baptist	0.9%
Episcopalian	0.7%
Methodist	0.4%
Lutheran	0.3%
Affiliates with Islam	0.2%
Judaism	0.0%

Waiola Church in Lahaina, Maui's first Christian church, was built in 1828. Queen Keōpūolani, one of the first ali'i to convert to Christianity, was laid to rest there as was her daughter, Nāhiena'ena.

Waiola Church. Joel Bradshaw, Wikimedia

The **Lahainaluna Mission School** was established in 1831, later known as the Lahainaluna Seminary, housed Hawai'i's first printing press where the first Hawaiian language bible was printed and published.

Lahaina Jodo Mission, a Buddhist temple in Lahaina, was established first as a private house in 1912, then moved to its present location in 1931. The large Buddha statue and temple bell commemorated the centennial anniversary of the first Japanese immigrants to Hawai'i.

Lahaina Jodo Mission. Wmpearl, Wikimedia

Maria Lanakila Catholic Church in Lahaina was the first Catholic church on Maui, built in 1928.

COST OF LIVING

Maui's overall cost of living (housing, food, transportation, utilities, health care, misc. expenses such as clothing, services, entertainment), not including state and local taxes, is 60.2% higher than the U.S. average.

Groceries costs 51.7% higher than on the U.S. mainland.

Housing costs 162.5% higher than on the U.S. mainland with a median home cost of $978,800. The average rent per month for a:

- studio apartment: $1530
- one bedroom: $1610
- two bedroom: $1990
- three bedroom: $2730
- four bedroom: $2940

Utilities cost 82.7% higher than on the U.S. mainland.

Transportation cost 11.8% less than on the U.S. mainland.

Maui County unemployment rate (2021): 4%

Paia storefronts. Travis Thurston, Wikimedia

MAUI COUNTY TAX RATES:

Sales tax rate:	4.0%	U.S. average is 7.3%
Income tax rate:	8.3%	U.S. average is 4.6%

The average income of a Maui County resident is $29,499 a year, the U.S. average is $28,555 a year.

The median household income of a Maui County resident is $64,567 a year. The U.S. average is $53,482 a year.

Kahului Airport. Forest & Kim Starr, Wikimedia

Visiting Maui

VISITOR ARRIVALS TO MAUI COUNTY (2021)

Total	Domestic	International
2,340,915	2,298,908	42,007

AVERAGE DAILY VISITORS (2021)

Total	Domestic	International
56,010	54,347	1,663

Number of hotels:	325
Number of hotel units:	17,688
Number of condominiums:	47
Number of condominium units:	3,726

	Hotel room occupancy	Average daily room rate
Wailea	56.4%	$831.06
Lahaina-Kā‘anapali-Kapalua	60.9%	$450.49
other Maui	59.3%	$638.62

belindah, Wikimedia

Haleakalā National Park (2021)	85,181 visitors

NUMBER OF NATIONAL AND STATE HISTORIC SITES (2022):

Listed Hawai‘i Register:	76
Listed National Register:	62

HOW FAR FROM HOME (OR SOMEPLACE ELSE)?

MAUI TO:	MILES	FLIGHT TIME
San Francisco	2,337.79	4h, 29m
Los Angeles	2,491.46	4h, 46m
Portland	2,558.31	5h, 2m
Seattle	2,647.69	5h, 12m
Las Vegas	2,693.25	5h, 12m
Vancouver, B.C.	2,681.06	5h, 52m
Anchorage	2,812.56	5h, 36m
Guam	3,900.15	8h, 19m
Tokyo	3,961.49	8h, 25m
Chicago	4,191.48	8h, 54m
Auckland, N.Z.	4,404.31	9h, 17m
Washington, D.C.	4,769.06	9h, 3m
Miami	4,776.81	10h, 4m
New York	4,905.22	10h, 19m
Sydney	5,113.17	10h, 43m
Manila	5,404.19	11h, 19m
Hong Kong	5,669.29	11h, 49m

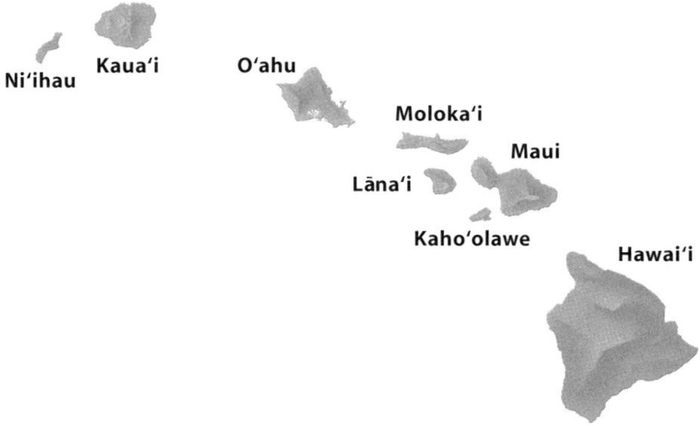

HAWAIIAN ISLANDS DISTANCES AND SIZES

ISLAND	DISTANCE (MILES)	FROM	AREA (MI²)	LENGTH	WIDTH
O'ahu	106.78	Maui	608	44	30
Kaua'i	224.20	Maui	553	33	25
Hawai'i		Maui	4,038	93	76
Kailua-Kona	79.84	Maui			
Hilo	106.30	Maui			
Moloka'i	50.85	Maui	261	38	10
Ni'ihau	259.48	Maui	73	18	6
Lāna'i	41.66	Maui	140	18	13

WEATHER

	AVERAGE TEMP COOLEST MONTH / WARMEST MONTH	EXTREME TEMP OF RECORD LOWEST / HIGHEST (2021)
Hana Airport	70.4 / 76.7 °F	60.1 / 87.6 °F
Haleakalā Summit	45.9 / 52.9 °F	35.1 / 69.6 °F
Kīhei	71.0 / 78.2 °F	60.1 / 87.6 °F
Lahaina	71.1 / 78.3 °F	60.3 / 87.8 °F

RAINFALL IN INCHES (2021)

Kahului Airport	17.01
Kīhei	12.95
Lahaina	14.18

CLIMATIC NORMALS, MEANS, AND EXTREME TEMPERATURES AT KAHULUI AIRPORT (2021)

	Temp (°F)
Normal daily maximum, annual	84.3
Highest daily maximum	97
Month and year of occurance	Sept 2019

Normal daily minimum, annual	67.4
Lowest daily minimum	22
Month and year of occurance	Jan 2004

Normal number of days with maximum 90°F and above: 17

NORMAL RELATIVE HUMIDITY, ANNUAL

8 am	74%
2 pm	58%

MEAN NUMBER OF DAYS (ANNUAL) WITH:

clear skies	130.5
partly cloudy skies	145.2
cloudy skies	89.5

MAJOR HURRICANES

	Date	Peak gusts
Estelle	July 22, 1986	55 mph
Olivia	Sept 8, 2018	130 mph
Douglas	July 20, 2020	130 mph

FAVORITE ATTRACTIONS

ATTENDANCE IN 2021	
Alexander & Baldwin Sugar Museum	4,743
Maui Ocean Center	257,570
Haleakalā National Park	853,181
Hana Cultural Center	150
Lahaina Restoration Foundation	7,039
Baldwin Missionary Home Museum	6,060
Wo Hing Temple Museum	979

Haleakalā Hawai'i State Archives

'Ohe'o Gulch (Seven Sacred Pools). Joe Parks, Wikimedia

OTHER FAVORITE ATTRACTIONS

1. Molokini Crater
2. Road to Hāna
3. Historic Pā'ia Town
4. Leilani Farm Sanctuary
5. Jaws surf break (Pe'ahi)
6. 'Ohe'o Gulch (Seven Sacred Pools)
7. Ali'i Kula Lavender Farm
8. Mākena State Park

Banyan Tree in Lahaina's Banyan Tree Park. Allie_Caulfield, Wikimedia

9. Kapalua Golf Resort
10. MauiWine
11. Lahaina's Banyan Tree
12. Ultimate Air Trampoline Park
13. Ho'okipa Beach Park
14. La Perouse Bay
15. Wai'ānapanapa State Park
16. Maui Arts and Cultural Center
17. Maui Zip n' Dip Tours
18. Feast at Lele
19. Maui Brewing Company
20. Kula Botanical Garden
21. Historic 'Īao Theater
22. Honolua Bay

Historic 'Iao Theater. Wikimedia

NONE HERE!

Happy Omissions

- Snakes
- Rabies—strict quarantine on incoming animals
- Cholera, malaria, small pox, yellow fever
- Billboards to spoil your view
- Hurricanes (seldom)
- Daylight Savings Time—no changings of the clocks in Hawai'i
- Car horns—most people drive with aloha and rarely use their car horn
- Private beaches—all beaches in the islands are public

Also to be missed

- Grass skirts—hula skirts have ti leaves. Hawaiian women wore tapa skirts (pā'ū)
- Hummingbirds—cross-pollination of pineapple blossoms would develop unwanted seeds in fruit
- Squirrels, racoons, chipmunks
- Many mainland chain retail stores and restaurants

MAUI HOLIDAYS AND CELEBRATIONS

- **February**–Kīhei celebrates World Whale Day and Maui's humpback whales with a parade and entertainment at Kalama Park with musical performances, keiki rides, food trucks, and craft booths.
- **April**–Maui Tropical Plantation hosts the Maui Agricultural Festival with farm-to-table cooking demos and samples, cooking competitions, and educational booths.

  East Maui celebrates taro with traditional Hawaiian food booths, arts and crafts, and farmers markets.

- **June** Kapalua hosts a wine and food festival complete with a golf tournament at the Kapalua Bay Golf Course, wine seminars and tastings, and cooking demonstrations.

On June 11, Lahaina and Central Maui host parades celebrating King Kamehameha Day along with events such as canoe races, horse races, carnivals, and performances.

The Maui Film Festival in Wailea kicks off with Taste of food festivals attracting celebrities from Hollywood and around the world, local filmmakers, artists, and film critics.

Obon season starts with festivals held at Buddhist Temples across the island featuring dancing, food, and drumming.

- **July**—For July fourth weekend, the Makawao Rodeo kicks off with a parade and features thrilling competitions for the state's top cowboys and cowgirls including bull riding, steer chasing, calf roping, bareback bronco riding, and more.
- **September to October**—Festivals of Aloha kick off, celebrating Native Hawaiian culture and traditions.
- **October 31**—Celebrate Halloween in Lahaina with a celebration on Front Street.
- **November**—The Maui Arts and Cultural Center hosts the Made in Maui Festival showcasing locally-made products.

Kā'anapali Beach. John P Salvatore, Wikimedia

MAUI BEACHES

Maui is graced with wildly diverse beaches that can be found along its 120 mile-long coastline due to the island's geological development with lava rock outcroppings, steep sea cliffs, and bordered bays. There are white, red, and black sand beaches, surfing and windsurfing spots, snorkeling and diving areas, and wide stretches perfect for sunbathing and picnicking.

Only a few beaches have lifeguards, so common sense must prevail. Watch out for shore breaks, rip currents, under tow, tsunami watches/warnings, and marine life. Many beaches have swiftly changing conditions and strong currents—do your research and don't underestimate the power of the surf.

Here is a list of some of the more well-known beaches on the island.

West Maui

Kā'anapali Beach–West Maui's most popular beach fronting a number of Kā'anapali resorts with Pu'u Keka'a, Black Rock, standing at the northern end. With three miles of white sand, it's a great spot for watersports enthusiasts.

D.T. Fleming Beach Park–Located across from Kapalua Golf Course, there's plenty of shade from ironwood trees, and picnic areas. Surf is especially strong in winter with rip currents in some spots.

D.T. Fleming Beach Park. KasugaHuang, Wikimedia

Kapalua Beach–Also known as Old Fleming Beach, this crescent-shaped beach is a good place for swimming, snorkeling, sunbathing, and picnicking.

Kapalua Beach. Christopher Michel, Wikimedia

Launiupoko Beach Park–Just one mile south of Lahaina, this family-friendly beach offers a natural pool, perfect for little waders, surrounded by lava rock walls. Watch out for sea urchins among the rocks. Lots of palm trees for shade in the picnic area.

Central Maui

Kanahā Beach Park–Close to Kahului and adjacent to the airport, this two-mile beach has the perfect conditions for windsurfing and kiteboarding.

Kanahā Beach Park. Forest & Kim Starr, Wikimedia

South Maui

Kama'ole Beach Parks I, II, and III–Considered Kīhei's best beaches, these three beach parks offer fine-grained golden sand with sunshine and views of the West Maui Mountains, Lāna'i, Kaho'olawe, and Molokini.

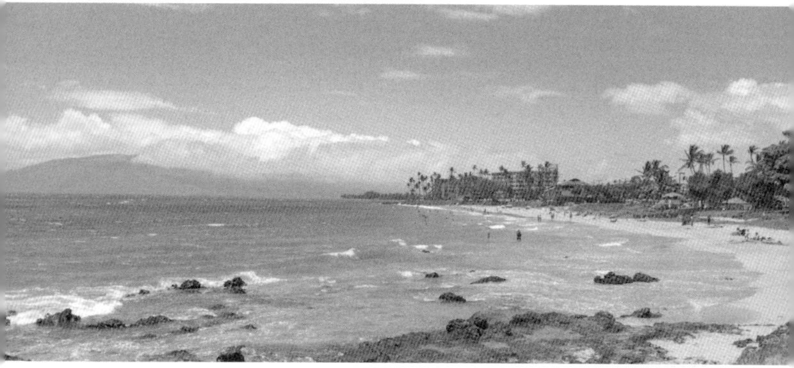

Kama'ole Beach Park. dronepicr, Wikimedia

Mākena Beach. dronepicr, Wikimedia

Keawakapu Beach–Between Kīhei and Wailea, this long, golden sand beach provides good swimming conditions, sunbathing, snorkeling, and spearfishing.

Mākena Beach–Also known as Oneloa Beach and Big Beach with 1.5 miles of golden sand extending as much as 100 feet wide, Mākena Beach is one of the largest on Maui.

Wailea Beach–Fronting Wailea's resorts gives this beach a resort feel. The public access and facilities are well-maintained as a result, yet the beach will be crowded with sunbathers, cabanas, and beach chairs.

Windsurfers at Hoʻokipa Beach Park. Christopher Michel, Wikimedia

North Maui

Pāʻia Bay–This long stretch of beach is for body boarders and body surfers with large waves–especially in winter.

Hoʻokipa Beach Park–A world-renowned windsurfing location where many competitions take place. But swimmers take heart, there are small sheltered areas for swimming along the shoreline as well as tide pools.

East Maui

Wai'ānapanapa State Park–A stunning black sand beach with a natural lava arch and a fresh water caves. Best to witness this beautiful beach from the shore as the rip current can be quite strong when surf is high.

Hāmoa Beach–This crescent shaped beach stretching 100 feet wide with white sands and popular shorebreak, is surrounded by sea cliffs.

Hāna Beach Park–This black/brown sand beach is often frequented by local picnickers and canoe clubs.

Lava tunnel at Wai'ānapanapa State Park. dronepicr, Wikimedia

MAUI MUSIC

Maui has inspired many musicians and composers and continues to energize local musicians and entice musicians from around the world to her shores. There are quite a few homegrown musicians that hail from Maui—Willie K, George Kahumoku, Jr., Amy Hanaiali'i Gilliom, Keali'i Reichel, and Anuhea—and quite a few transplants who can be seen playing music around town in small, unassuming venues. Here is just a small sampling of songs featuring Maui.

He Aloha No Ku'u 'Aina

Written by Cody Pueo Pata, the song celebrates the island of Maui.

Puamana

Written by Irmgard Farden Aluli, the song is an ode to her family home in Lahaina.

Nahiku

Written by Mathew Kalalau and performed by Kaiolohia Funes Smith, the song is about the sweet smelling 'awapuhi (yellow ginger) that grows in Hāna.

Yellow ginger flowers. James Brennan Molokai, Wikimedia

Kuahiwi Nani

Written by Alice Namakelua, the song pays homage to Haleakalā.

Going to Hāna Maui

Written by Peter "Pekelo" Cosma in 1995, the song features slack key guitar and is about driving home to Hāna.

Maui Waltz

Written by Bob Nelson in 1969 and performed both by Loyal Garner and The Brothers Cazimero, the song reminisces about a lost love.

Haleakalā Hula

Written by Alice Nāmakelua in 1941 to accompany the Maui float in the Kamehameha Day parade.

Lahaina Luna

Written by Kui Lee in 1966, the song includes the phrase Maui nō ka 'oi and describes watching the moonrise over Lahaina.

The Hasegawa General Store

Written by Paul Weston in 1961, the song became popular after it was performed by Pua Alameida on the radio show "Hawaii Calls."

Hasegawa General Store. Lechhansl, Wikimedia

Ho'okipa Paka

Written by Alice Johnson in 1937, the song is an homage to Ho'okipa Beach Park where one can rest in the shade and watch the surfers.

'Ulupalakua

Written by John Pi'ilani Watkins in 1947, the song describes 'Ulupalakua on the southwestern slopes of Haleakalā as the home of the cowboy with cool mountain air scented with ginger.

Maui Hawaiian Sup'pa Man

Written by Del Beazley and Mel Amina and performed by Israel Kamakawiwo'ole, this song retells legends of Maui including pulling up the island chain with his magic fish hook, slowing the sun, and finding fire.

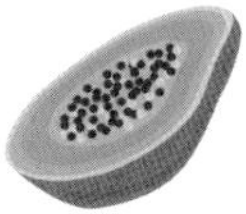

FOODS

Maui is where Hawaiian Regional Cuisine was created and the island continues to inspire chefs and farmers who strive to promote farm-to-table cooking.

Many of the farms on Maui offer tours and invite visitors to come try their locally-grown produce. One can also visit wineries, breweries, farmers markets, fish markets, plate lunch places, high end restaurants featuring multi-course dining experiences, bakeries, and specialty dessert shops. Maui has proven itself to be a diverse source of culinary experiences that attract food tourists who want to learn more about the culture through its food. With its rich agricultural history, it's no wonder Maui continues to lead in the culinary field.

DINING TREATS

Hawaiian Fresh Fish

- **'Ahi**–yellowfin tuna
- **Aku**–bonito, smaller tuna
- **Mahimahi**–light white fish, dolphin fish (not the porpoise which is also called dolphin)
- **Ono**–wahoo (mackerel family); another delicious white fish
- **'Ōpakapaka**–pink snapper
- **'Ōpelu**–mackerel, scad
- **Ulua**–pompano

Hawaiian Kau Kau—Lū'au

- **Pūpū**–appetizer
- **'Opihi**–raw shellfish, limpet
- **Laulau**–pork and fish steamed in ti leaf
- **Lomilomi salmon**–salad of salmon, tomatoes, onions, mixed together
- **Limu**–fresh raw seaweed

- **Chicken long rice**—bean thread noodles with chicken and green onions
- **Kimchi**—Korean pickled cabbage
- **Kālua pig**—pork baked in an imu (underground oven)
- **Poi**—mashed taro root
- **Haupia**—coconut pudding

Taste Tests—Special Foods

- **Azuki**—small red beans cooked, sweetened, and mashed as fillings
- **Bamboo shoots**—for meat and noodle dishes
- **Bean sprouts**—in many Asian dishes
- **Breadfruit**—steamed, boiled, fried, baked, or mashed, baked with coconut cream
- **Chinese peas**—flat pods lightly cooked
- **Daikon**—Japanese long radish
- **Dasheen**—Japanese for taro
- **Gobo**—Japanese burdock
- **Lily buds**—in duck and pork dishes
- **Lotus root**—in meat dishes

- **Lūʻau**–taro leaves cooked with milk, coconut milk, or fat, sometimes with chicken or octopus; always served at a party
- **Malasadas**–Portuguese round doughnuts, no hole
- **Miso**–fermented soybean, rice, and salt paste for soup
- **Nori**–paper-thin sheets of matted seaweed to wrap around vinegared rice with fish and vegetables
- **Saimin**–noodles in Japanese dishes
- **Sashimi**–small slices of raw fish in soy sauce
- **Shoyu**–soy sauce
- **Sukiyaki**–thin-sliced beef with lightly-cooked vegetables
- **Tempura**–batter-dipped meat, deep-fried
- **Teriyaki**–meat marinated in soy sauce, broiled
- **Tofu**–soybean curd; used with soy sauce in Asian dishes
- **Water chestnuts**–crisp slices for Chinese meat and vegetable dishes
- **Yam bean root** (chop sui potato)–Chinese stir-fry dishes

Island Treats

Crack seed—preserved, seasoned, chewy fruits with cracked seeds, whole seeds, or seedless; also candied squash or coconut; watermelon or pumpkin seeds; pine nuts; dried cuttlefish, squid, scallops, abalone, or octopus

TAKING AWAY PLANTS, FRUITS, AND FLOWERS

- **No restrictions**—ripe coconut, pineapple, macadamia nuts, flowers—except for gardenias, jade, mauna loa, any pea family
- **Must be fumigated**—avocado, banana, lychee, papaya; fumigated fruit available at airport and some dealers
- **Mango**—must be pitted, frozen, or cooked
- **No plants in soil**
- **Orchids**—shops carry pre-inspected plants
- **No citrus**—all items checked at Airport Agricultural Inspection

LANGUAGE

Standardized by missionaries in 1820s, only twelve-letter alphabet; five vowels, seven consonants: h, k, l, m, n, p, w.

Pronunciation—Vowels

a—ah—as in hale (house)—hah-lay
e—ay—as in kāne (man)—kah-nay
i—ee—as in ipo (sweetheart)-eepoh
o—oh—as in ʻono (good)—oh-noh
u—ue—as in pūpū (snack)—pooh-pooh

Common Words

Activities

hana—work
hui-club, organization
hukilau—group net fishing
kōkua—help
lomilomi—massage

Clothing

haori—Japanese coat
holokū-gown
lavalava-Samoan skirt
malo-loincloth
muʻumuʻu—long, loose dress
pāpale-hat
pāʻū—sarong-type skirt

Conditions

ho'omalimali–flattery, sweet talk
huhū–anger
pilikia-trouble
wikiwiki–fast, hurry

Descriptions

akamai–clever, smart
auwe–alas
nani–beautiful
nui–big
'ono–delicious
pau–done, finished
pupule–crazy

Directions

kona–leeward, south, south wind
makai–toward sea
mauka–toward mountain

People

ali'i–chief, royalty
haole–white person; foreigner
kahuna–priest in old Hawai'i, expert practitioner
kama'āina–native-born or long-time resident
kāne-man
keiki–child, little one
kupuna-grandparent, ancestor
malihini–stranger, foreigner
paniolo–cowboy
tūtū grandmother
wahine-woman

Religion

akua-god
'aumakua–family god
Kanaloa–god of deep sea
Kāne–giver of life
Kū–main god
lani-heaven
Lono–god of agriculture

mana–spirit, power
Pele–goddess of volcano

Things

ʻaʻā–rough, stony lava
hale–house
hīmeni–missionary hymns
hula–a dance
imu–underground oven
kāhili–feather-decorated royal standard
kai-sea
lānai–porch
lau–leaf
lua–hole, depression, toilet
mele–song, anthem, or chant
pāhoehoe–smooth or ropey lava
pua–flower
puka–hole, opening
pūneʻe–couch
wai–water

Expressions

da kine (pidgin)–whachamacallit
Hauʻoli lā hānau–Happy Birthday
Hauʻoli Makahiki Hou–Happy New Year
Mele Kalikimaka–Merry Christmas
mahalo nui–many thanks
Pehea ʻoe?–How are you?

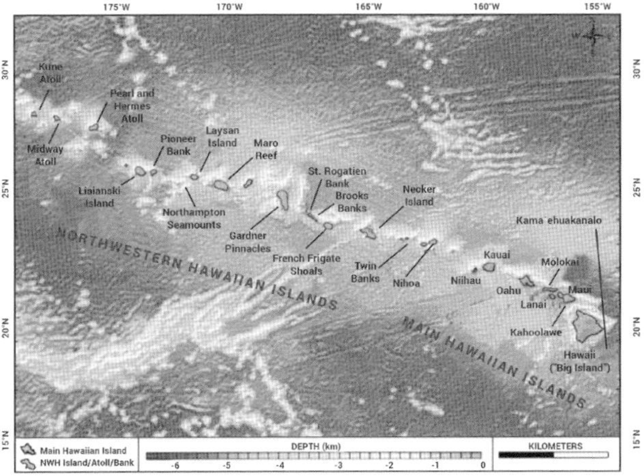

Hawaiian Archipelago. SOEST at University of Hawai'i at Manoa.

Natural History

The Hawaiian island chain stretches 1,600 miles from Kure atoll, 1,200 miles northwest of Honolulu, to the Island of Hawai'i. It is the longest chain of islands in the world.

It started about 25 million years ago and continues with eruptions on the Island of Hawai'i.

Haleakalā, making up the east half of Maui, rose 750,000 years ago, last erupting around 210 years ago. The west half of Maui rose 1,300,000 years ago.

FACTS & FIGURES

Geography

County seat: Wailuku

Size: 771.99 square miles; 48 miles in length, and 26 miles in width

Distance from O'ahu: 70 miles

Coastline: 120 miles long

Beaches: 81 beaches, over 30 miles

Channels

	Width	Depth
'Alenuihāhā (Hawai'i-Maui)	29.6 miles	6,810 feet
'Alalākeiki (Kaho'olawe-Maui)	6.7 miles	822 feet
'Au'au (Lāna'i-Maui)	9.5 miles	252 feet
Pailolo (Maui-Moloka'i)	8.8 miles	846 feet

Summits

Haleakalā is 12,575 acres and 3,028 feet deep.
Haleakalā (Red Hill) is 10,023 feet high.
Haleakalā (Kaupo Gap) is 8,201 feet high.
Pu'u Kukui is 5,788 feet high.
'Īao Needle is 2,250 feet high.

Waterfalls

Honokōhau cascades 1,120 feet down and is 500 feet wide. Waihiʻumalu cascades 400 feet down and is 150 feet wide.

Major Streams

Kalialinui-Waiʻale Gulch	18 miles long
Palikea Stream	7.8 miles long
Waiheʻe River	50 miles long
Honokōhau Stream	9.4 miles long
ʻĪao Stream	5 miles long

ʻĪao Stream in ʻĪao Valley State Park. Larry D. Moore, Wikimedia

- As of December 31, 2021, Maui has 98 bridges. Honokahua is the longest at 600 feet; Uaoa is the highest at 79 feet.
- Road to Hāna (Hāna Highway): 64.37 miles long, 600 curves, 54 bridges.
- Haleakalā Crater Road is 10.11 miles long.

ANIMALS

Hawaiian green sea turtle–Honu, a threatened species, can be found across all the islands swimming above reefs or basking in the sun on the beach.

Hawaiian monk seal–The endangered Hawaiian monk seal, endemic to the islands and one of the rarest mammals in the world, can be seen on all the islands, including Maui, resting on the beach or swimming out at sea.

Humpback whale–Every year from November to April, humpback whales migrate from the cold waters off Alaska to Hawai'i to give birth and nurse their young in warmer waters.

'I'iwi–The Scarlet Honeycreeper is a threatened species whose population has severely declined in recent years due to habitat loss, invasive species, and avian disease spread by mosquitos. Ninety percent of the entire population can be found on East Maui and on the windward slopes of Hawai'i island.

HarmonyonPlanetEarth, Wikimedia

Manta Ray–Olowalu Reef off West Maui's coast is home to a cleaning station where over 350 manta rays congregate to have smaller fish clean them of parasites. Manta rays, hāhālua in Hawaiian, are fairly tame. They do not have teeth or tail stingers, unlike Sting Rays, and can grow close to 3,000 pounds and a wingspan of 23 feet. Their distinctive physical characteristic are the front cephalic flaps that funnel water and food into their mouths.

Maui Parrotbill–This native honeycreeper, also endangered, can now only be found at high elevations in East Maui. They are yellow with olive green wings and tail, with strong, curved bills used to split branches to extract insect larvae. Once widespread on Maui and Moloka'i, there are currently an estimated 500 birds left.

Zach Pezzillo, Maui Forest Bird Recovery Project

Nēnē–Endemic to the Hawaiian Islands, Hawai'i's endangered state bird can be found on the slopes of Haleakalā and here and there across Maui in the West Maui Mountains, around Makawao, and in Central Maui.

Pueo–This endangered Hawaiian owl is endemic to the islands and plays an important role in Hawaiian legends and myths. They can be seen flying along the slopes of Haleakalā and gliding over Upcountry pastures.

FLOWERS, PLANTS, AND TREES

Maui's varied landscape—with high and low elevations, wet and dry areas—enabled a wide variety of flowers, plants, and trees to grow. From the canoe plants Polynesians first brought to the islands to the plants introduced by missionaries, industrialists, and scientists, Maui is ripe with both invasive and native species all vying for space—not a small number of which have since become extinct. The island's ecosystem is both fragile and strong and Maui's people are working hard to restore, maintain, protect, and conserve as many native species as they can.

African Tulip Tree—Introduced in the 1800s by a botanist, this rapidly growing tree with flaming orange flowers, has been threatening native vegetation in Maui's lowland forests. They can be found along Hāna Highway.

Forest and Kim Starr, Wikimedia

'Ama'uma'u Fern—Endemic to Hawai'i, they grow abundantly at higher elevations like Haleakalā and are the first to grow after new lava flows.

Banyan–One of the largest banyan trees in the world is in Lahaina, brought from India in 1873 to commemorate the fiftieth anniversary of the missionaries who arrived on Maui. Since then it has grown from eight feet tall to an impressive sixty feet tall with branches that stretch out over 200 feet.

Breadfruit–Brought to the islands by Polynesian voyagers, this high-yielding plant became a key staple food in their diet. All parts of the tree were used, from the wood, the sap, and the leaves.

Ginger–A wide variety of ginger grow all over Maui–from the iconic red torch ginger, to Kahili ginger, to the white and yellow ginger lilies used to make fragrant lei.

L-R: Torch ginger Vinayaraj; ***Kuranda ginger*** Sheba_Also; ***and white ginger*** Emőke Dénes, Wikimedia

Hala (Pandanus)–Hala can grow well in salty or sandy soil, in hot and windy areas, and at low elevations. They bear fruit and flowers.

Heliconia–These tropicals come in a variety of funky shapes, sizes and colors–some stand up straight like Bird of Paradise, and some hang, like Lobster Claw.

Jacaranda Tree–Springtime is announced in Upcountry Maui by the blooming jacaranda trees that line Kula and Puakalani Highways. It's possible Portuguese plantation workers introduced jacaranda to the island in the early 1900s.

Koa–One of the largest trees in the islands, reaching up to 115 feet, koa was traditionally the most valued tree in Hawai'i.

'Ōhi'a–'Ōhi'a range in size from a shrub to a 100-foot tree and grow at sea level and in high elevations, in dry lava flows and in lush rainforests.

Protea–Kula, in Upcountry Maui, is known for its flower farms and is perfectly suited to grow protea. Originally from South Africa, there are over 1,600 varieties of protea.

Silversword–Indigenous to Hawai'i, in fact, found only in Hawai'i, these unique plants can be seen scattered along Haleakalā's slopes.

POLYNESIAN IMPORTED PLANTS
THEIR MAINSTAYS OF LIFE

Bamboo–one of man's most useful plants; for boat parts, containers, dishes, fishing equipment, food, furniture, hats, implements, mats, musical instruments; fastest growing; recorded at 47.6 inches in 24 hours; 1,250 species–tallest 125 feet; dies after flowering at 50 to 100 years old.

Banana–matures in 14 months; only one bunch per tree; new trees grow from suckers around base.

Breadfruit–ripens October to March; weighs up to 10 pound; eaten baked, boiled, broiled, or glazed.

Coconut–about 5 pounds; best drink is "water" from green ones; milk made by squeezing grated meat from young nut through cloth.

Gourds–provide containers, musical instruments.

Hau–true hibiscus–yellow flower changing to apricot color, then dark red.

Kukui–oil for stone dish lamps; candles of nuts strung on coconut fibers; torches of nuts stuffed in bamboo; bark to dye tapa, fish nets; baby food of ground roasted nuts with poi; mouthwash from sap; oil from green nuts for aching muscles; laxative from 1 to 3 green nuts.

Lauhala (Hala, Pandanus, Screw pine)–also called "walking trees," because roots spread out and down from trunk; leaves (lau) for thatch, mats, baskets, purses, sandals, fans; fruit like pinepple in shape only; not eaten.

Lipstick plant–bright yellow dye from scarlet seeds.

Milo–small yellow hibiscus-like flowers; wood for food bowls because it has little flavor.

Paper mulberry (Wauke)–bark for tapa cloth.

Sugarcane–energy source for long voyages.

Taro (Kalo)–large leaf; root cooked as food and to make poi.

Ti–green leaf variety sacred; to keep away evil spirits from temple and home; good luck symbol; root steamed as food; also used to make liquor; as food, helped prevent scurvy for sailors; leaves for laulaus, hula skirts, wrappers, thatch, table decorations.

Sweet potatoes, yams, tumeric, and **wild ginger** were also brought to Hawai'i by the Polynesians.

TROPICAL FLOWERS

Anthurium (Flamingo flower)—waxlike, some 500 varieties; white to red, some orange and green; last 3 weeks.

Bird of Paradise—orange and blue—like brilliant bird's head.

Gingers—about 1,300 species—47 genera—bloom March to December.

Blue—purplish-blue upright spikes, but not a true ginger.

Crepe (Malay)—bell-shape, fringed white flowers.

Kahili—loose, erect yellow-red heads

Red—rich red overlapping bracts, upright

Shell—dropping clusters, shell-like; delicately shaded in white and yellow with red dashes.

Torch—largest—with red head-like overlapping scales; also pink.

White (Ginger lily)—mothlike with delightful fragrance.

Yellow—mothlike but smaller than white; used for traditional leis.

Heliconia—hanging and upright varieties with series of richly colored bracts and large leaves (of banana family).

Lobster claw—upright series of alternate pointed red bracts in clawlike form.

Hanging–string of dark red pointed bracts, small yellow flowers protruding; also one with red keels edged with green and yellow.

Pink and green–upright bracts, pinkish center bordered by light yellow and green.

Night-blooming Cereus–rich-scented white and yellow blossoms in evening on heavy cactuslike wall vine; June and October.

Orchids–thousands of varieties.

Cattleya–large blossoms in many colors, forms, and combinations.

Cymbidium–delicately tinted waxlike; long-lasting.

Cypripedium–lady slipper type

Dendrobium–cane orchids; blossoms in sprays; variety of colors.

Epidendrum–loose blossom head of bright little flowers; variety of colors.

Miltonia–pansylike in pink, lavender, purple, and white.

Oncidium–variety of forms; many like butterflies and insects; mostly bright yellow with brown markings.

Phalaenopsis–moth orchids, so-named because of size and shape; very showy

Vanda–varies in size and color combinations of blue, brown, pink, red, white in dots, streaks, and veins.

HAWAIIAN MEDICINAL PLANTS

Pandanus tectorius (Hala). Forest and Kim Starr, Wikimedia

Aloe—excellent for swelling, burns, sunburns; used in some prepared medicines.

'Ape—used as a burn cure; leaves for headaches or neuralgia.

Breadfruit ('Ulu)—milky sap for cuts and cracked skin.

Hala (Pandanus)—for tumors; flower for constipation.

Herbaca—tea served as birth control.

Hinahina-leaves brewed into tea for diabetes.

Kukui (Candlenut)—used for thrush, internal disease, asthma, tuberculosis; flower for diarrhea.

Laukahi—leaves for debility and diabetes.

Noni—for swelling, thrush, diabetes, tumor, dizziness, high blood pressure; juice of fruit for diarrhea, typhoid, or paratyphoid.

Castor bean. Vinayaraj, Wikimedia

Bird of Paradise. Tiraspolsky, Wikimedia

WATCH OUT! POISONOUS PLANTS!

Azalea—all parts

Be Still (Yellow Oleander)—all parts

Bird of Paradise—seed pods

Castor bean—all parts, especially seeds

Coral plant—seeds

Crown flower—milky juice

Lantana—berries

Oleander—all parts

Pencil plant—all parts

Poinsettia—leaves, stem, sap

Crown flower. Adityamadhav83, Wikimedia

History

TIMELINE

1500s	Chief Pi'ilani begins construction of the Alaloa, or King's Highway, which is completed by his son, Kihapi'ilani.
1736	Kahekili rules over Maui.
1768	Queen Ka'ahumanu is born in a cave called Pu'u Ka'uiki in Hāna.
1786	The first Westerner, Admiral Jean-Francois de Galaup, Comte de La Pérouse, sets foot on Maui.
1790	Kamehameha I battles and defeats Kahekili's army at Kepaniwai in 'Īao Valley. Captain Simon Metcalf of the *Eleanora* kills 100 Hawaiians in Olowalu Massacre.
1795	Kamehameha I conquers Maui for a second and final time.
1802	Kamehameha I moves his army to Lahaina in preparation for attack on Kaua'i and constructs the Brick Palace.

1819 The first north Pacific whaling ship stops in Lahaina. Ka'ahumanu becomes kuhina nui, or Queen Regent, when Liholiho, Kamehameha II becomes king, and continues on through Kamehameha III's reign.

1820s Commercial sugar operations begin. Lahaina becomes the capital of the Hawaiian Kingdom.

1823 Reverends William Richards and Charles Stewart, Maui's first Protestant missionaries, arrive in Lahaina.

1824 Ka'ahumanu creates Hawai'i's first codified body of laws modeled after Christian ethics.

1825 Kauikeaouli is proclaimed King Kamehameha III at age twelve upon Liholiho's death. Queen Ka'ahumanu is baptized.

1828 Maui's first stone church, Waiola Church, is built in Lahaina.

1831 Lahainaluna Mission School is established. It is home to Hawai'i's first printing press, Hale Pa'i, where English and Hawaiian Bibles, scholarly books, and newspapers are printed.

1835 Reverend Jonathan Green establishes the Wailuku Female Seminary at the entrance to 'Īao Valley.

1840	Lahainaluna scholars, headed by David Malo, write Hawai'i's first constitution.
1849	California's gold rush increases demand for Kula potatoes and other crops.
1851	Mormon religion established at Kealahou.
1852	Chinese immigrants arrive as labor for sugar plantations.
1856	Honolulu businessman James Makee builds Rose Ranch, later known as 'Ulupalakua Ranch.
1862	Pioneer Mill Company plants cane in Lahaina. Wailuku Sugar Company commences business.
1869	Henry Perrine Baldwin and Samuel Thomas Alexander purchase twelve acres of East Maui land to plant sugar cane.
1878	Completion of Hāmākua Ditch leads to the expansion of the sugar industry. Claus Spreckels acquires 40,000 barren acres in Central Maui, establishes Hawaiian Commercial Company, and constructs his own irrigation system with the help of a German engineer, Hermann Schussler. Portuguese recruited as plantation laborers.

1879	The Kahului and Wailuku Railroad transports sugar from Wailuku to Kahului Harbor.
1880s	Germans arrive as plantation workers.
1881	Norwegians and Swedes arrive. Electricity comes to Maui.
1888	Haleakalā Ranch is incorporated and Henry P. Baldwin becomes shareholder and President.
1895	Japanese laborers arrive.
1898	Alexander & Baldwin purchase Hawaiian Commercial & Sugar Company.
1899	Italian sugar workers arrive.
1900	Hawai'i is annexed to the United States. Robert Wilcox is elected as the territory's first delegate to Congress. Puerto Ricans and Okinawans arrive as plantation workers. *The Maui News* begins publication. Bubonic plague breaks out in Kahului.
1901	African Americans arrive. Pioneer Hotel (now Inn) opens.
1902	Hawaiian Commercial & Sugar Company's Pu'unēnē mill begins operation.

1903	Koreans arrive. Maui Agricultural Company forms from Haiku and Pā'ia Plantations.
1905	Maui County forms is founded to include five districts: Lahaina and Lāna'i, Wailuku and Kaho'olawe, Hāna, Makawao, and Moloka'i.
1907	Spaniards arrive to work on plantations. Writer Jack London and his wife, Charmian, visit Maui.
1909	Russians recruited for plantation labor. Filipinos arrive.
1912	Pineapple planted in West Maui on Honolua Ranch, later to become Baldwin Packers.
1919	Lahaina's business district is destroyed in a fire.
1929	Interisland air transportation is launched.
1930	A massive fire devastates Pā'ia town.
1932	Maui Pineapple Company forms from Haleakalā Ranch and Maui Agricultural Company's holdings.
1940	Pu'unēnē Naval Air Station is built.
1941	Kahului Harbor is shelled by Japanese submarines. Maui placed under martial law.

1943	Kahului Naval Air Station established.
1944	Camp Maui becomes home to the Fourth Marine Division with its main base in Hā'iku. Maui's beaches are used for practice landings and training.
1947	Hotel Hāna Maui opens to guests.
1948	Maui Agricultural Company merges with Hawaiian Commercial & Sugar Company.
1950	Kahului's Dream City welcomes its first residents.
1951	The Kahului Shopping Center opens.
1956	The first Makawao Rodeo is organized.
1959	Hawai'i becomes a State.
1962	The Royal Lahaina Beach Hotel opens, the first in Kā'anapali. Hāna Highway is paved.
1966	Kahului Railroad ceases operation.
1969	Hippies arrive and settle in south Maui at Oneloa Beach introducing marijuana culture.
1970	Development of Wailea begins.

1971 Maui Mall opens.

1972 Ka'ahumanu Shopping Center serves first customers.

1978 Kapalua Bay Hotel opens to guests.

1983 United Air Lines provides direct service from the mainland to Maui.

1991 Hawai'i Regional Cuisine, Inc. is developed on Maui by twelve island chefs who form the association in order to advocate for locally sourced ingredients and inform the world about Hawai'i's unique culinary history and future ambitions.

1998 Republican Linda Lingle narrowly loses the race for Maui mayor. In 2002, she becomes Hawai'i's first female governor and first Republican governor in forty years.

2008 Moloka'i Ranch ends operations.

2009 Maui Land & Pineapple closes Maui Pineapple Co. after ninety-seven years in business.

2010 W.S. Merwin, a Maui resident since 1976, is named the seventeenth U.S. Poet Laureate by the Library of Congress. Hali'imaile Pineapple Co. Ltd. is established to continue growing pineapple on Maui Pineapple Co. land under the Maui Gold brand.

2012 Oracle CEO and billionaire, Larry Ellison, purchases the bulk of the land on Lāna'i from Castle & Cooke, Inc. for an undisclosed price estimated at more than $500 million.

2016 Maui's first mayor, Elmer Cravalho, passes away.

Sea Link of Hawaii, Inc., a ferry service between Maui and Moloka'i, ends service after nearly three decades.

The Hawai'i Supreme Court approves construction of the Daniel K. Inouye Solar Telescope on the summit of Haleakalā. Kilakila o Haleakalā, a group of Native Hawaiian cultural practitioners, fights the University of Hawai'i at Mānoa for six years over the construction permit.

Hawaiian Commercial & Sugar Co. closes its mill, ending commercial sugar cane farming on Maui after 146 years of operation.

2017 Two medical marijuana dispensaries open on Maui–Maui Grown Therapies and Pono Life Sciences Maui. Pharmlabs Hawaii, Maui's first medical marijuana laboratory, is certified to test the purity of the drug which means dispensaries no longer have to send cannabis samples to O'ahu for testing.

2018 Alexander & Baldwin sells 64 square miles of Maui sugar land to Mahi Pono, a venture between California-based Pomona Farming and Canada's Public Sector Pension Investment Board.

2021 Mahi Pono announces it has planted, on former sugar lands, 600,000 citrus trees, 300,000 coffee trees and 21,000 papayas–nearly a million trees in all.

2022 Moloka'i and Maui struggle with severe overpopulation of axis deer which are overrunning farmland, emergency disaster declared by governor.

MAJOR HISTORICAL FIGURES

Pi'ilani–In the sixteenth century, Chief Pi'ilani ruled the area from Hāna to the six bays on West Maui's coast, referred to as Honoapi'ilani. To facilitate travel, Pi'ilani began construction of the King's Highway–a hand-constructed, lava rock-paved and walled road connecting the west and the east. His son, Kihapi'ilani continued construction after his father's death making Maui the only island with an ancient road encircling its entirety.

Kahekili–In 1736, Chief Kahekili ruled Maui from Wailuku with designs to unify the islands. In 1790, Kamehameha, a warrior from the Island of Hawai'i who shared Kahekili's ambitions, confronted Kahekili and his army at Hānawana Bay in East Maui. Successful, Kamehameha and his warriors then sailed to Kahului and forced Kahekili and his warriors into 'Īao Valley. There, with the aid of Western firearms, Kamehameha's army killed most of Maui's forces at what is called the Battle of Kapaniwai, or Battle of the Dammed Waters.

Admiral Jean-François Galaup, Compte de la Pérouse–In 1786, the French explorer La Pérouse was the first Westerner to set foot on Maui. La Pérouse had sailed from Easter Island with two ships—the *Astrolabe* and the *Boussole*—in search of the Hawaiian Islands with particular interest in Maui.

Captain Simon Metcalf—A British American merchant fur trader, Captain Simon Metcalf, anchored his brig, the *Eleanora*, off the southern coast of East Maui in 1790. A Hawaiian man named Kaopuiki and a few accomplices stole a small boat and killed the sailor on watch. In retaliation, Metcalf fired on innocent Hawaiians in a trading canoe and on shore and left for Olowalu, where Kaopuiki was said to be from. At Olowalu, Metcalf lured 200 canoes to his brig for trading and fired on them without warning, killing more than 100 Hawaiians and injuring 150.

Kamehameha I—In his quest to unify and rule all the Hawaiian Islands, Kamehameha I battled Kahekili at the Battle of Kapaniwai in 1790, which was the beginning of the end of Kahekili's reign. In 1794, Maui was Kamehameha's and in 1802, Kamehameha and his family move to Lahaina to prepare his army for a Kaua'i attack. There he built the Brick Palace, the first Western-style house in the islands, for Ka'ahumanu.

Keōpūolani–High ali'i, or chiefs, were considered divine, and a child born of a brother-sister union of high chiefs was the most sacred. Keōpūolani was the daughter of such a union. Keōpūolani had three children with Kamehameha, two boys and one girl, cementing the royal Kamehameha line.

Queen Ka'ahumanu–Ka'ahumanu, the daughter of Nāmāhāna whose lineage was of Maui chiefs, and Ke'eaumoku, a rival chief from the Island of Hawai'i. As a teenager, she married Kamehameha I and became his favorite wife, and in 1802, moved with him and their family to Lahaina. She was also a strong advocate for education and instructed the building of schools on the windward side of Maui.

Original artwork by Louis Choris. Reproduced photographically by J.J. Williams with charcoal work by J. Ewing. Hawai'i State Archives

Liholiho, Kamehameha II–Kamehameha II became king in 1819 upon the death of his father. The whaling industry was booming and the ports of Honolulu and Lahaina were becoming rowdy with sailors, bars, and brothels. Kamehameha II moved the capital to Maui, just before the first Maui missionaries arrived.

Kauikeaouli, Kamehameha III–Only twelve years old when he became king several months after his brother's death, Kamehameha III ruled with the help of Ka'ahumanu until her death in 1832. Kamehameha III lived in Lahaina from the 1820s through the 1840s. Lahaina missionaries helped shape the government and Kamehameha III advocated for the importance of education. Lahainaluna Seminary opened in 1831 and Hawai'i's first constitution was drafted by Lahainaluna scholars 1840 which led to the Great Mahele.

David Malo–A Lahainaluna scholar, David Malo helped draft the 1840 Constitution of the Hawaiian Kingdom. He helped translate the Bible into Hawaiian and wrote about Hawaiian religion and culture, published in book form titled *Mo'olelo Hawai'i,* or *Hawaiian Antiquities.*

Henry L. Chase, Hawai'i State Archives

Reverend William Richards–In 1823, Reverend William Richards and his wife, Clarissa, arrived in Lahaina on the Royal Yacht, *Cleopatra's Barge.* He established the Lahaina mission (Lahainaluna Seminary) and worked to translate the Bible into Hawaiian with David Malo and others and helped draft the 1840 Constitution of the Hawaiian Kingdom.

Reverend Dwight Baldwin–A missionary physician, Dr. Dwight Baldwin arrived in 1835 with his wife from Waimea. They built a home in Lahaina, which still stands today as a museum, and raised six children there–many of whom stayed and shaped Maui's economic future.

Reverend Jonathan Green–Before settling in Wailuku in 1833, Reverend Jonathan Green and his wife arrived in Honolulu from Connecticut in 1828. In 1836 they founded a girl's boarding school, the Wailuku Female Seminary.

Reverend Lorrin Andrews–Lahainaluna's principal and sole instructor in its first years, Reverend Lorrin Andrews arrived in 1827. He published the first Hawaiian *Ka Lama Hawai'i* (The Hawaiian Luminary), an early Hawaiian dictionary, and the first Hawaiian grammar book after constructing a printing house, Hale Pa'i, which housed a printing press.

Hawaiian Mission Children's Society

Betsey Stockton–Born into slavery in 1798, Betsey Stockton became the first single American woman missionary sent overseas. As a paid domestic servant for Reverend Ashbel Green, Stockton learned of the mission to Hawai'i and requested to go. Stockton founded the first school for commoners (non-ali'i) in Lahaina in 1824 and within two years, 8,000 students attended almost 200 island schools. Stockton trained native Hawaiian teachers who took over for her after she left the islands in 1825.

Captain George Vancouver–After sailing with Captain James Cook in the HMS *Resolution*, Vancouver returned to the islands in 1793. Between 1973 and 1974, Vancouver attempted to bring peace between Maui, Hawai'i, and Kaua'i, acting as an ambassador between Kamehameha, Kahekili, and Ka'eo, the chief on Kaua'i. In addition to his offers of peacemaking, Vancouver brought the first cattle to Maui which become a significant industry for the island and helped shape Maui's cultural identity.

Governor Hoapili–As governor of Maui, he advocated for schools and education requiring all children over four years old to enroll in school and declaring literacy as a prerequisite for marriage. In 1826, he ruled all marriages on Maui should be Christian and built the first stone church, Waine'e Church (now known as Waiola Church) in Lahaina. From 1824 to 1840, Governor Hoapili improved the King's Highway.

Hawai'i State Archives

Edward Bailey–Edward Bailey arrived with his wife, Caroline, in 1837. They both taught at the Wailuku Female Seminary, and Bailey designed and helped build

Ka'ahumanu Church in Wailuku and a water-run sugar and wheat mill in Wailuku which eventually merged with Wailuku Plantation.

Charles William Dickey—C.W. Dickey was the architect of many famous structures throughout the islands and is credited for developing Hawai'i's distinct architectural style. Among the buildings Dickey designed on Maui were Wailuku Elementary School in 1904, Makawao Union Church in 1917, the Baldwin Bank in 1931, and Kula Sanitorium in 1937, which housed quarantined tuberculosis patients.

Helio and **Petero Koaeloa**—Fathers Barnabe Castan, Father Modest Favens, and Brother Jean Marie Gabriac established Maui's first Catholic mission in 1846.

James Makee—Honolulu businessman James Makee purchased a large piece of 'Ulupalakua in 1856 to raise cattle, plant sugar cane and cotton, and create a paradise retreat. When blight doomed his sugar cane fields, he converted everything to ranch land and 'Ulupalakua Ranch became Maui's largest ranch.

Samuel Thomas Alexander—The son of early missionaries, Reverend William Alexander and his wife, Mary Ann. In 1864 he married Martha Eliza Cooke, daughter of missionary Amos Star Cooke who founded the Castle & Cooke company. In 1869 he purchased land in eastern Maui with his friend, Henry Perrine Baldwin, which led to Pā'ia Sugar Mill and the formation of Alexander & Baldwin.

Henry Perrine Baldwin–The son of early missionaries, Reverend Dwight Baldwin and his wife Charlotte. Baldwin was as instrumental in the Hāmākua Ditch project. Baldwin became owner of *The Maui News* in 1905 and was active in government from 1887 to 1904.

Claus Spreckels–Known as "The Sugar King" before Henry Baldwin took the title, Claus Spreckels established his own sugar plantations on Maui in 1878, founding Spreckelsville, a company town in Kahului for his Hawaiian Commercial & Sugar Company. In 1880, Spreckels purchased the newspaper *Pacific Commercial Advertiser* which later became known as *The Honolulu Advertiser* and financed the first ship in the Matson Navigation Company.

Library of Congress

Patsy Matsu Takemoto Mink–Born in Hāmākua Poko on Maui in 1927, Patsy Mink became the first Asian American woman elected to Congress in 1965. She served six consecutive terms and a total of twelve terms.

George Jarrett Helm, Jr.—A Native Hawaiian activist and musician born on Moloka'i, George Helm worked with the group Hui Alaloa in 1975 to protect Kaho'olawe from U.S. Navy bombing exercises.

Linda Lingle—In 1990, Linda Lingle ran against Hawai'i State Speaker of the House of Representatives Elmer Cravalho and was elected Maui County's youngest and first female mayor. In 2002, Lingle was elected Governor of Hawai'i.

U.S. Navy

Larry Ellison—Co-founder and former CEO of Oracle, Larry Ellison purchased ninety-eight percent of the land on Lāna'i from Castle & Cooke, announcing in 2017 his plans to develop sustainable, computer-driven hydroponic greenhouses on the island as well as transform the Lodge at Kō'ele into a high end, health-retreat resort.

Elmer Cravalho—From 1969–1979, Elmer Cravalho served as Maui's first mayor following statehood. As the descendant of Portuguese immigrants, Cravalho was born in Pā'ia in 1926. While mayor, he was involved in much of Maui's economic development.

Sources

Maui

"The History of Maui." Nov 29, 2016. https://sailmaui.com/the-history-of-maui/#:~:text=The%20name%20'Maui'%20is%20said,named%20after%20the%20demigod%2C%20M%C4%81ui

Fun Facts About Maui

Cheung, Marcie. "Facts about Maui You Probably Didn't Know" Hawaii Travel with Kids, August 24, 2022. https://hawaiitravelwithkids.com/facts-about-maui/

Sewell, Alli. "Do You Know These 20 Fun Facts About Maui, Hawaii?" December 9, 2011. https://www.destguides.com/united-states/hawaii/maui/maui-hawaii-facts

"15 Facts About Maui." Oct 18, 2022. https://www.madeinmauicountyfestival.com/media-news/maui-facts

"20 Fun Facts About Maui Hawaii to Know Before You Go." October 27, 2021. https://www.nothingfamiliar.com/facts-about-maui/

"Ten Things You Didn't Know About Maui." Updated: February 4, 2014. https://www.mauiinformationguide.com/blog/ten-things-you-didnt-know-about-maui/

Precious Land

"Land Use and Ownership." The State of Hawaii Data Book 2021. https://files.hawaii.gov/dbedt/economic/databook/db2021/section06.pdf

Agriculture

"2017 Census of Agriculture County Profile: Maui County, Hawaii." United States Dept. of Agriculture. https://www.nass.usda.gov/Publications/AgCensus/2017/Online_Resources/County_Profiles/Hawaii/cp15009.pdf

Religions

"Best Places to Live in Maui County, Hawaii." https://www.bestplaces.net/county/hawaii/maui

https://www.gohawaii.com/

Cost of Living

"Economy in Maui County, Hawaii." https://www.bestplaces.net/economy/county/hawaii/maui

"County Economic Conditions." Research & Economic Analysis Department of Business, Economic Development & Tourism. https://dbedt.hawaii.gov/economic/qser/county/

Visiting Maui

"Population." The State of Hawaii Data Book 2021. https://dbedt.hawaii.gov/economic/databook/db2021/

How Far From Home?

"Distances from Maui." https://www.distance.to/Maui

www.travelmath.com

Weather

"Geography and Environment." The State of Hawaii Data Book 2021. https://dbedt.hawaii.gov/economic/databook/db2021/

Other Favorite Attractions

"Top 50 Maui Activities & Things To Do." https://www.prideofmaui.com/blog/activities/top-10-maui-attractions

Natural History

"How Old is Hawaii?" Updated on September 14, 2021. https://www.mauihawaii.org/how-old-hawaii/

History

Bartholomew, Gail and Bren Bailey. *Maui Remembers: A Local History.* Honolulu: Mutual Publishing, 1994.